AF211728

JILL MORTY

SMART MONEY HABITS

The Ultimate Guide on Money Saving Tips, Learn All the Best Practices and Proven Strategies on How You Can Save Money in Everyday Life

Descrierea CIP a Bibliotecii Naţionale a României
JILL MORTY
   SMART MONEY HABITS. The Ultimate Guide on Money Saving Tips, Learn All the Best Practices and Proven Strategies on How You Can Save Money in Everyday Life / Jill Morty – Bucharest: Editura My Ebook, 2021
   ISBN

JILL MORTY

SMART MONEY HABITS

The Ultimate Guide on Money Saving Tips, Learn All the Best Practices and Proven Strategies on How You Can Save Money in Everyday Life

My Ebook Publishing House
Bucharest, 2021

101 Money Saving Tips

1. Use solar powered light fixtures.

There are lots of light fixtures today that can be powered by the sunlight. In using them, you would be able to save lots of money, since your electricity bills would go down. All you have to do is to shop for these items at your local store, or even through the web. Some of these items are even very easy to install and are available in DIY kits.

2. Walk towards the grocery store.

The price of gasoline these days continue to go up, which is why it is a good idea to come up with ways to lessen your vehicle usage. One of which would be to walk towards the grocery store, especially if it is just a few blocks away from your place. Make it fun by walking with your spouse, so that aside from saving money, you both can also shed some weight.

3. Open your windows instead of turning on the fan.

When it is hot, you may want to turn on the fan or even your air conditioning system, in order to improve the temperature at your place. To save money, instead of using them, you can always open up your windows. By doing that, you can benefit from fresh air, aside from saving money. To make it cooler, you can always put some ice in front of the fan if you want to.

4. Turn off your computer when not in use.

There are lots of people today who turn on their computers at the beginning of the day, and only turn it off before sleeping at nights. If you are one of them, then you should turn it off, prior to stepping outside your place. By doing that, you can ensure that you would be consuming lesser amounts of energy. Aside from that, it can also prolong the life of your computer.

5. Clean your own car.

The cost of having your car washed through a car washing station on a weekly basis, can easily pile up over the months. Thus, if you are going to wash your own car, then you would be able to save lots of money. Aside from that, it can also provide you the exercise that you need, in order to stay as fit as you can be.

6. Turn off the television.

Becoming addicted to the television is one of the things that can cause your electricity bills to soar higher. Thus, you need to turn it off, when you are not watching. Aside from that, you should also minimize the times that you try to watch TV, when you are actually doing another thing.

7. Turn off the lights at your place when you leave.

You may feel more secure in leaving your place while the lights are turned on. However, it can be one of the factors that affect your energy bills. Thus, you should turn the lights off when you leave. If you want, you can still leave just a single light on, so that you would feel secure when you go out.

8. Ride the bus instead of using your car.

If you are going somewhere, which is not possible to reach by merely walking, then you should ride the bus, instead of using the car. Riding a bus or a train can only cost you a few dollars, compared to filling up your car with lots of gasoline. Just prepare earlier, and take note of the schedule of the bus, so that you won't be late.

9. Be healthy.

The cost of medicines today continue to go up, especially when it comes to antibiotics. To ensure that you won't have to reach for your pocket to buy them, you need to maintain your health. To achieve that, you should get enough exercise on a regular basis. Aside from that, you should also take a multivitamin supplement in conjunction with a healthy diet.

10. Don't turn on the water faucet at its maximum level.

When you take a bath, there is no need to turn on the water at its maximum level, especially if you are not in a rush. Turning it at higher levels can make your water bills soar high. Thus, if you take control of it, then you should be able to save some money by conserving water more effectively.

11. Try to enjoy leftovers.

When you eat at restaurants, cook up some delicious meals for a family gathering or prepare for a birthday party, you can be sure that you would have a bunch of leftovers inside your refrigerator after. Heating them up for your meals instead of throwing them away could save you a lot of money.

12. Cook your own meals.

Cooking your own meals could help you save lots of money. This is because buying the ingredients for a certain recipe is definitively more affordable, than eating out in restaurants or fast food chains. Just make sure to cook healthy meals, so that you can also ensure that you are getting the nutrients you need.

13. Buy basic things in wholesale prices.

There are lots of basic things that a person needs, and buying it in retail prices can pile up the cost. Thus, it is best if you buy them in bulk, since that would give you a chance to purchase them in wholesale prices. In doing this, you would be able to save lots of money, aside from the fact that you can have good supply of your needs.

14. Shop online.

Shopping online can give you an opportunity to save some amounts of cash. If you do your research, you would find out that most items found through the internet are more affordable than those that are sold in local stores. The reason behind this is that, online stores have lesser overhead expenses. Thus, shopping the modern way should help you save up some cash.

15. Buy used items.

Buying used items compared to buying those that are brand new is definitely more affordable. Thus, if you want to save money, then you should begin shopping around for used products. To find them, you can always go through the internet, visit garage sales, or check out some local auctions.

16. Buy an alternative.

When you do your research, you would find out that lots of products that you need have available substitutes. Thus, you should consider purchasing the substitutes of the items that you need, which are more affordable, but can offer you the same thing. For example, instead of buying a high end branded item, you can check out its equally competitive alternative, which can offer the same features at a lower price.

17. Look for coupons.

There are lots of coupons available today, which you can access through the internet. These coupons can offer you discounts on certain fast food chains, restaurants, as well as in local stores. All you have to do is to sign up for the websites that offer them, and follow the simple instructions provided.

18. Take advantage of sale, especially after the holidays.

Taking advantage of sale, especially those that are offered after the holidays can help you save lots of cash. For example, in most cases, decorations would become very affordable after the Christmas season. Thus, if you want to save money, you can always purchase them for the following year.

19. Credit card promotions.

Credit card promotions are offered every now and then, in which it can provide you a way to save some money through gift cards, gift checks, or discounts on certain stores and restaurants. Some can even offer a cash back option, for a certain amount of credits used, or when you purchase from certain stores.

20. Fix things up yourself.

Before tossing out an item, you should see if you can repair it yourself first. By doing that, you would be able to save money by not having to purchase a new one. To fix something up, you can always ask your friends for tips regarding it. Aside from that, you can also check out some troubleshooting tips through the internet.

21. Avoid spending through credit cards.

Spending through credit cards is one of the best ways to pile up your debt. Thus, if you want to save more money, you should purchase on cash basis only. Save the credit cards for emergency situations only. Every item you purchase with the use of your credit card can add more to your existing debt and your monthly surcharge; thus, it is time that you leave them at home when you go out to shop.

22. Gaming at nights.

If you and your friends are quite fond of going out at nights, especially on weekends, then you should invite them for a gaming night at your place. This would help you all in saving lots of money. All you have to do is to take out your favorite board game, buy some snacks and drinks, and enjoy a good time at your place, without spending lots of money in bars or coffee shops.

23. Watching movies at your place.

If your family wants to spend some time with you by watching a movie in town, you should consider watching one at your own house. Renting a video at a shop near your place should do the trick. Pair it up with some popcorn and sodas, and your family would have a great time with you, while you are not worrying about the total cost.

24. Swaps are good.

Swapping your things that you are not using anymore for a new item, is one of the ways of saving money, when it comes to acquiring something new. Swapping can be done through the internet, with your friends, or with certain shops. You can swap your shoes, books, music, movies, games, gadgets, and more, for items that you want to have so that you won't have to spend a dime in getting it.

25. Buying magazines at a newsstand.

If you are quite fond of certain types of magazines, buying them at the newsstand should be avoided. This is because they are usually priced too high when you purchase them from these types of stores. To save money, you can always subscribe directly to the magazine. Aside from that, check out their websites, since they might even offer e-magazines, which you can conveniently download into your computer for free or for a very affordable price.

26. The lottery.

If you are fond of playing the lottery, you should seriously think about your odds of winning it. There is very less likelihood that you would hit the jackpot in the lottery, and each time you play it, you are actually spending more cash. Thus, if you simply want to be entertained, then you should consider playing at a casino, since the cost is pretty much the same, the odds would be better, and it can provide you with more entertainment.

27. Traveling.

In traveling, one of the best things that you can do in order to save huge amounts of money is to book way ahead of time. This is true, especially if you book online. Lots of airlines are actually offering discounts for early bookings today. Aside from that, you should also keep in mind that booking a vacation package is also more affordable, than booking your hotel, flights, and cars separately.

28. Your travel times.

To save up some money, you should be flexible when it comes to your traveling times. For example, in booking flights, if you are not in a hurry, red-eye flights are actually good to book in terms of saving cash, although you may not want your children traveling late. Aside from such types of flights, traveling to certain vacation spots during off-season can also be a good idea, when it comes to saving on costs.

29. Going from one building to another.

If you are at a city center, where you are anticipating to move from one building to another to look for certain types of items, then you should park your car at a garage or parking area, which is located centrally. This way, it would allow you to leave it there, instead of driving it around town and consume more gasoline. With that, you would be saving more money, and even get some exercise.

30. Car rental insurance.

If a car rental company offers you an add on car rental insurance, you should stop for a moment, and think about your own auto insurance. Most auto insurance companies today provide policies, where your auto insurance coverage would also apply to your rental car. Thus, if this is the case, then you should decline the offer. However, it is still best to call your insurance provider for that, just to make sure.

31. Riding a bike.

When you are on your way to a place where it is a bit far for a walk, then you should make use of your bike. Biking can prevent you from using more fossil fuel, which can harm the planet, aside from costing you money. With that, you should always ride your bike, so that you consume lesser amounts of fuel, and save more money.

32. Talking to a travel agent.

If you are not getting anywhere in trying to book more affordable fights and accommodations online, you should know that many travel websites have travel agents working for them. They are usually reachable through their 800 numbers on a 24 hour basis. Thus, giving them a call should provide you with the assistance that you need, in order to find the package that you really want.

33. Having an affordable vacation.

During the holidays, people usually go to distant places to spend their vacations on. However, if your finances is quite tight or you simply want to save money, then you should consider having a vacation at the city where you are living it. By doing that, you would be able to rediscover your place. Aside from that, since you won't be going out of the place, you won't have to spend quite a hefty some of money for your flights.

34. Using the ATM.

It is always best to use your bank's ATM machine, whether you want to process a withdrawal, fund transfer, or even just checking for your balance. This is because when you do these things in another bank's ATM machine, you would be charged by that bank, as well as your own bank for certain fees.

35. The card's annual fee.

There are credit cards today that offer free annual fees, while some do not. Credit card companies that charge annual fees may have added features into their cards. However, in most cases, such features are not very applicable to lots of people. Thus, it is best to choose cards that won't charge you annual fees, so that you can save more money on a yearly basis.

36. Rate reductions.

If you are carrying a balance in your card and it has been like that for quite some time, then try to negotiate for rate reductions. There is a good chance that your credit card company would agree to this. This is because they don't want to risk more defaults, since it is bad for their business.

They would rather ask lesser amounts of money from you, than suffer the consequences of more defaults.

37. Bundling insurance policies.

There are certain insurance providers today, which can offer not just auto insurance policies, but also homeowners, and other forms of insurances. If you want to save some money, you should ask your provider for possible discounts if you bundle your policies. When you do that, aside from saving money, it would also become more convenient for you, since you won't have to deal with paying different providers.

38. Take advantage of deductibles.

If you want to reduce your monthly insurance premiums, then you should recheck your insurance coverage for possible deductibles. Deductibles are the amount of money that you need to shoulder in an event of an accident. Your premium would decrease when you have it, since part of the risk would be transferred to you from the company.

39. Paying insurance premiums.

When you pay your insurance premiums, you should do it way ahead of time. This is because insurance companies can offer you with more discounts when you pay it before the due date. Thus, it is best if you ask your insurance provider about this, so that you would be able to take advantage of it.

40. Have a savings account in more friendly banks.

There are certain banks these days that can charge you so many fees that you won't even get the chance to earn any kind of interest. One of the fees that are quite common for some banks is called the maintenance fees. Thus, if you read your bank's booklet and found this term, then you should consider switching banks as soon as possible.

41. Take care of your credit card debt.

One of the things that can add more to your monthly expenses is your credit card debt. This is because the higher your debt becomes, the more you need to pay in terms of its interest. In other words, you may end up paying for the interest each month, without even touching the principal amount you owe. Clear your credit card debt by applying for a low cost loan, so that you can breathe easier.

42. Cutting your home phone bills.

Landlines or home phone services usually cost more than their VOIP counterparts. Thus, you should consider switching to a VOIP phone service and just maintain your mobile phones. Aside from that, you should also check with your local phone service provider, if they can provide you with the most basic service to cut down on costs.

43. Go to the grocery store after eating and not before.

When you go to a store to shop for groceries, it is always best to do it after grabbing a snack, or eating lunch. This is because shopping in groceries when you are hungry can make you purchase food items, which you really do not need. In most cases, when you get home from shopping and eat lunch, you would realize later on that you have gone over your budget, for taking in too many food items.

44. Shopping for clothes.

In buying your own clothing, you may have a tendency to purchase those that are heavily advertised by celebrities. Designer label clothes are very expensive. Although they are good in terms of quality and design, you can actually find lots of products today, which are equally good but are more affordable. Thus, avoid such types of clothing, so that you can save some money.

45. Take advantage of online auction sites.

When you take a look around your own house, you may realize that you have lots of used things, which you are not using anymore. If these items are still in good condition, then you should sell them in online auctions sites. Earning more money is also a good way to saving more. Aside from that, while you are earning online, you can actually get rid of the clutter and have more space in your house.

46. Do It Yourself.

You should become a DIY person if you want to save more money. By becoming one, you no longer have to hire a carpenter in fixing something at your own place. Aside from that, you also won't have to hire someone to clean your backyard, especially if you gain more knowledge in gardening. Becoming a DIY person will open lots of opportunities for you not just to save more money, but to earn more as well.

47. Travel insurance.

Prior to getting a travel insurance, you should decide to go on a trip first. Thus, if you have previously acquired an annual insurance, then you should not renew it, unless you are going to travel soon. If you are unsure, then only renew it, when you are about to book another trip for your family.

48. Get more quotes.

When it is the time of the year to renew your auto insurance, you should not hesitate in shopping around for the most affordable rates. A good way of doing this is to get free quotes from different insurance providers. Before you decide to switch to another insurer though, make sure to consider the coverage they can provide, to be on the safe side.

49. You can always say no.

If your kids are quite fond of telling you what they want at the grocery store or at the toy store, then you should practice saying no to them. Aside from that, you should also learn to say no to your friends, if they want you to out with them for drinks. Saying no would not just feel liberating, but it can also help you save some dough.

50. Keeping up with appearances.

If you have a tendency to buy something that you saw your friend or neighbor has recently bought, then you should cut that costly habit. This is because you may end up buying lots of things you don't need. Aside from that, you don't even know how your neighbor got it; and, they might even have used their credit cards for it.

51. Trading your car.

Having a new used vehicle is not such a bad idea, especially if you want to save some cash. You should also consider this, if the car that you currently have piles up your expenses by consuming more gas, and offering little space for your family. There are lots of car supermarkets these days, which can offer you a quality used vehicle that has a price that is just a fraction of the brand new one. Check them out, so that you can save more cash.

52. Shopping items on sale.

If you just happen to be in a store because you have free time, and you found items that are on sale, then you might be tempted in acquiring them immediately. However, before you make a drastic move, try to think about whether you really need the item or not. Although the item may cost only half of its original price, you still should not buy it if you don't really need it.

53. Your gym membership.

In order to have a healthier body, you may be visiting the gym on a regular basis. However, if your busy schedule prevents you from visiting it at least thrice a week, then you should cancel it. With your hectic schedule, you should workout at your own place from now on. Aside from saving more time, you can also save some money since you won't have to deal with membership fees.

54. Cut down your drinking habit.

Aside from the fact that drinking can cause negative effects to your health, it actually adds up on your monthly cost of living. If you are used to drinking a bottle or two of your favorite beer each night, you should cut it down to just a couple of beers only on weekends. By doing that, you are doing your body a favor, as well as your pocket.

55. Quit smoking.

Smoking is one of the leading causes of certain types of diseases all around the world. Aside from that, cigarettes also continue to become more and more expensive these days. Thus, you should find ways to quit it. When you quit smoking, you can lessen your risks to certain diseases, smell good, and save some money along the way.

56. Use the internet.

If you are in need of a new recipe, a new guide to playing the guitar, or a new manual for self- development, you no longer have to go to the bookstore and spend lots of cash for it. What you can do is to access websites for the information that you need. Aside from offering you informative articles about the topic you are interested in, you can also find lots of eBooks on the web that are for free.

57. Extended warranties.

Extended warranties are usually available for popular electronic devices. They are usually offered so that you would have a warranty that extends for more than just a year. Before you take advantage of it though, you should stop and think if you really need it. In most cases, a warranty for six to twelve months is already enough. Just make sure to choose an electronic device that is made in good quality, so that you won't have to worry about extended warranties.

58. Eat lesser amounts of meat.

When you compare meat products to vegetables, they are more expensive, aside from the fact that they are often associated with fats. Thus, it is best to eat more vegetables instead. However, since you need meat for your source of protein, you should opt for chicken without its skin, since they are more affordable.

59. Eat in a slower pace.

When it comes to eating, you can save more money and lose weight by eating slower. This is because when you eat slow, you will have a tendency to eat less, since your stomach would take a certain time to send a message to your brain that it is already full. Thus, in eating slower, you won't just enjoy a fitter you, but you can also enjoy more savings since you consume lesser amounts of foods.

60. Bring your own lunch.

If you don't have the time to go home and eat lunch, you should cook your own food and bring it with you. By doing this, you won't have to spend lots of money in eating at restaurants or fast food chains. Aside from saving lots of money, you can also ensure that you stay in good health, since you would be the one to prepare it.

61. Avoid the vending machine.

When you want a snack and you visit the vending machine for it, most likely, you would be paying a lot more for the foods that you eat, than if you were buying them from the grocery store. Therefore, the next time you purchase goods from the grocery, make sure to include your snack food items. By doing that, you can simply bring them with you, each time you report for work.

62. Making a list for the grocery.

When you are shopping at a grocery store, chances are you would end up going over your budget if you won't bring a list with you. Thus, it is a good idea to make a list of all the things that you really need. Aside from that though, make sure to take note of the prices of the grocery items, so that you already have an idea how much you are going to spend when you buy your groceries.

63. Buying medicines.

In buying medicines, the factor that can affect their prices are their brands. Thus, if you want to save money, then you should stick to generic brands. These generic medicines are actually equally effective as its high end counterparts. Just take note of the name of the medicine prescribed by your doctor and not the brand, so that you can save some cash.

64. Visiting the coffee shop.

If you simply love coffee and you often find yourself going to coffee shops for it, then you should learn how to brew your own coffee soon. There are lots of coffee making products available in the market today, which can allow you to make cups of delicious coffee in just a matter of minutes. Purchase one soon and you would be able to enjoy your favorite cup of coffee, without having to go out of your place and spending more money.

65. Go with water.

When you are thirsty, whether you are at a movie theater or at the mall, you should skip soda, beer, or juice, and stick to water. This is because water is more affordable than the other drinking beverages, and in some places, it can even be offered for free. Aside from saving more money by drinking water, it can also help you stay fit, since it is not loaded with calories.

66. Collect reusable bags.

When you have a bunch of reusable bags at your place, then you can bring it with you when you buy your groceries. There are certain grocery stores these days, which can offer you discounts, tokens, or coupons, if you are going to being your own bag for your purchased goods. By doing that, you won't just be saving money, but you could also be saving the world by using lesser plastic bags.

67. Driving at nights.

Whenever you are driving at nights, you can actually save up some money by opening your car windows. By doing that, you would not have to turn on your air conditioner, and save up some gas in the process. With lesser gasoline consumed on a regular basis, you would be able to save more money.

68. Make sure your tires are properly inflated.

Making sure that your tires are properly inflated can prolong its life and save you some money in the process. Aside from that, it can also ensure that handling your car would be easy. Moreover, when the tires are properly inflated, you can also be assured that your car's fuel efficiency is at its maximum levels.

69. Get your car checked regularly.

Having your car go through routine maintenance actually offers a lot of benefits to you. Aside from making sure that your car is in top condition, it could also prevent damages, which can cost you a lot of money. Just make sure to find a reliable mechanic, so that he won't always tell you to replace something, just to make a quick buck.

70. Free parking.

When you go around town, you may find that lots of places require payment for parking, especially those that are near certain landmarks. However, if you are patient enough, you should be able to find a place that offers free parking. You may have to walk a few blocks towards your destination for it, but it would be worth it, especially if you practice this regularly.

71. Opting for a more basic insurance coverage.

To save up some money in terms of your insurance premiums, you can always tell your insurance provider to drop your collision and comprehensive coverage. This is a wise move, especially if your car is quite old. However, you need to be aware that dropping the said items from your declarations page would mean that you would be responsible for the cost of repairs to your own vehicle, whenever you are involved with an accident, in which you are the at-fault party.

72. Choosing services you really need.

Each year, you should evaluate what services you really need and what services you don't need. You should ask yourself whether you really need to have cable television, landline, magazine subscriptions, and such. Try to check which services you really need to have a decent way of living, and stick only with them. Drop the other ones you don't need, so that you can save money.

73. Play online games.

If you have an internet connection at your place, it is far better to play online games, instead of purchasing more video games for your gaming console. There are lots of online gaming sites today, which can offer you the kind of entertainment that you want for free. With that, you won't have to pay for video games that are pretty expensive, which can help you save more money.

74. Don't use your dryer.

In washing your clothes, you may have gotten used to utilizing the dryer of your washing machine to dry your clothes up. However, if you want to save money, then you should line dry your clothes instead. This simply means getting yourself a clothesline or a rack where you can dry your clothes on. By doing that, you are lengthening the lifespan of your machine, aside from minimizing energy consumption.

75. Turn off your electric stove earlier.

Whenever you are using your electric stove to cook a meal, you should make it a practice to turn it off earlier than usual. This is because the plate on your stove usually stays heated even when the power is turned off. Thus, if you turn it off a few minutes early, then it can still continue to provide heat to your recipe.

76. Focus on your collection.

Lots of people like to have a collection of certain things, which they consider as a hobby. Some people like to collect caps, while others enjoy collecting bags. If you are one of them, then you should think whether the things you are collecting can really provide you with what you need. If not, then you should try to stop your costly habit. Instead, you should try to sell your collection, so that you can add more money to your savings account.

77. Customer rewards programs.

There are grocery stores and even bookstores today, which offer customer rewards programs. If the store that you usually purchase items from offer it, then you should sign up with them.

Although it takes some time to rack up some points, it can still provide you with something, which can help you extend your budget. Aside from that, some of these reward programs can also give you coupons and discounts on certain items.

78. Check out your credit card points.

Lots of credit card companies today offer rewards in relation to the points that you have collected whenever you use your card. If you have gathered enough points, you should check out the available items that you can redeem it for. Aside from items though, some companies may also agree to waive some fees associated with your account in exchange for the points.

79. Personalize your gifts.

Whenever you hand out gifts for birthdays, Christmas, and such, it is always best to personalize them, in order to increase its value. Aside from making the present more meaningful though, personalizing gifts can also offer you a way to save up some cash. Thus, make use of your imagination, so that you can save up some money, while making your friends happy.

80. Let time pass by.

Whenever you find yourself longing to purchase something new, such as a new gadget, a new pair of pants, or a new pair of shoes, you should let a couple of weeks pass by, before making up your mind about it. In most cases, you can find yourself losing the urge to buy the item that you want, especially if you really don't need it.

81. Spend less money but have more fun.

If you are the kind of parent who wants to see their kids having fun, there is actually no need to spend lots of money for it. Instead of taking them to rides or at the malls for shopping, you can actually make ordinary stuffs around your house interesting and fun enough for your kids. You can do some paper tossing, do origami, play hide and seek, and such so that you can all have some fun, without spending money.

82. Eat healthier meals.

Avoiding highly processed foods is actually something that offers more than just health benefits. It can also help you save up some money, since they usually cost more than when you prepare your own meals. Preparing your own meals can help you save money, since you can easily load it up vegetables, which are more affordable than meat.

83. Don't leave the door of the refrigerator open.

Leaving the door of your refrigerator open for a long period of time can cost you lot of money, due to using up lots of energy. This is because whenever you open your refrigerator, it could lose a certain amount of its cool temperature, and will have to try to attain it again. Thus, tell all the members of your family about this, so that you can minimize your energy consumption.

84. Your car's air filter.

Cleaning your car's air filter will take you a long way when it comes to saving money. This is because a clean air filter can improve your vehicle's fuel efficiency. With that, you can be assured that your gasoline consumption would be maintained at reasonable levels. Just check out your car's manual in doing it, so that you can clean the air filter soon.

85. Making your own things.

Making your own things can actually help when it comes to saving more money. When you bake your own cake or bread, you would soon realize that it is actually a lot more affordable in purchasing the ingredients for it and making it, than buying them from the bakeshop. Thus, learn making your own things soon, so that you can save more money in the process.

86. Finding relief from stress.

If you need to relieve yourself from stress, there is no need to spend lots of money for it. As long as you know some meditation techniques or yoga, then you wouldn't have to go to spas or massage parlors to relax. Aside from that, you can even just sit or lie down and listen to soothing music in order to get over a stressful day at work.

87. Do a routine check on your appliances.

You should regularly check your appliances in order to save more money. When you constantly check your appliances, you would be able to see if there are dusts on certain parts of it, such as the vents, the backs, and such. If you keep the appliances well cleaned, you can improve their efficiency and prolong their life.

88. Club memberships.

If you have a country club membership or a gym membership that you actually are not using, then you should cancel it. By doing that, you would be able to save some amounts of cash on a monthly basis. There is no need to worry about canceling them, since you can always renew your membership whenever you want to.

89. Wash your hands properly.

Cleaning your hands thoroughly after going to the comfort room, or touching different types of things like money, books, among others, is one of the best ways to prevent diseases to affect you. Keeping yourself from viruses and bacteria can help in saving money, since you won't have to deal with medical bills and medicine costs.

90. A gift does not have to be an item.

Providing your friend with a service that they really need can be a very meaningful gift, instead of giving them the usual gift item. For example, you can actually offer to wash your friend's car and wax it, instead of purchasing a gift item for him. Aside from that you can also offer to baby- sit for your friend, so that she can go out with her spouse.

91. Online accounts.

If you saved your credit card information on your online accounts so that you can easily purchase items that you want, then you should remove them soon. This is because this can give you a very easy way to overspend or go over your budget. Once you remove them, whenever you need to purchase something, you will have to look for your credit card information, which can take up some of your time.

92. Buying a car wisely.

Whenever you want to buy a brand new car, a couple of factors you want to consider would be the car's fuel efficiency and reliability. When you focus on these factors, it can actually save you lots of money in the long run. Thus, you should do your research about the cars you are considering purchasing soon, so that you can have the one that can help you save more money.

93. How to prevent shopping by impulse.

Making impulse buys, especially if you use your credit card for it can pile up your debts. To ensure that this is not the case, whenever you have the urge to purchase something, you should spend around a minute or two in thinking about whether you really need it or not. If not, then you simply have to let go of the urge, and save your hard earned cash.

94. Taking care of your debts.

If you want to save more money, you should take care of your debts very soon. One of the best ways to do it is to come up with something, which can remind you about it regularly. You can set a reminder about it through your phone, or come up with a visual reminder, so that you would become more consistent in hitting your goals regarding your debts.

95. Eating a full breakfast.

When you eat a full breakfast, you won't just be having the energy that you need to get through the day easily, but it can also save you some money. This is because it can control your unnecessary cravings during lunch and dinner. Aside from that, a full breakfast is often more affordable than large meals during lunch and dinner; thus, you won't have to deal with a huge expense for it.

96. What to do when you want to buy clothes.

Whenever you have the urge to buy new clothes, you should check out your closet first. If you find out that there are lots of clothes you have that you have not used for the past months, then you should bring them in front. By doing that, you would actually feel like you already have newer sets of clothes; thus, it can prevent you from shopping for unnecessary clothing.

97. Gain the support of your family.

If you want to save more money, you should tell your family all about it. When you do that, you can actually gain their support. If your whole family supports you, you can all work out together in order to minimize your costs. They can all help in minimizing energy and water consumption. Aside from that, they could also understand better if you won't be eating out as often as you usually do.

98. When your computer is not working.

If your computer is not working as fast as it usually does, or it is not functioning normally, you should not contact your equipment's manufacturer for it immediately. This is because, they might send someone to repair it, and charge you lots of cash. Instead, you should try to troubleshoot it yourself it at first. Do your research about it through the internet, such as accessing websites or online forums, so that you can save money and learn new things.

99. Take up gardening.

Gardening can be fun, aside from the fact that it can help you save more money. When you already have a garden, you won't have to spend extra cash for cabbages, tomatoes, oranges, and other fruits and vegetables, since you can conveniently grow them yourself. By doing that, on top of saving money, you can also ensure that you are consuming organic food items.

100.   Check your mobile phone bill thoroughly.

To save more money, one of the best ways to do it is to check your phone bill for the services that you have enrolled it with. Try to carefully evaluate these services, so that you can properly decide whether you really need them or not. To get rid of some, all you need to do is to contact your service provider and tell them about it.

101.   Make your own wine.

If you love to drink wines so much, then you may have already spent lots of money in purchasing bottles of your favorite drinks. There are actually affordable wine making kits available in the market today, and they usually come with everything, which include the ingredients. By using such kits, you no longer have to purchase expensive wines, since you can already make them yourself.

Printed by Libri Plureos GmbH in Hamburg, Germany